JUNIOR
BIOGRAPHIES

Rita Santos

HAILEE STEINFELD

ACTRESS AND SINGER

Enslow Publishing
101 W. 23rd Street
Suite 240
New York, NY 10011
USA
enslow.com

WORDS TO KNOW

a cappella Sung without instruments.

cast To hire an actor for a role.

casting call A request for performers who fit a certain role.

debut First time in public.

dialect Language of a certain area that is different from standard language.

director The person who is charge of making a movie.

EP Extended play record. It has more than one track, but it is not an album.

hobby An interest or activity done for pleasure.

inspire To move someone to do something.

interior designer A person who designs the inside of houses or buildings.

trio A set of three.

CONTENTS

Hailee Steinfeld

CHAPTER 1

TRYING NEW THINGS

Hailee Steinfeld was eight years old when she decided to try acting. Her cousin got a part in a commercial. This **inspired** Hailee to try acting as well. She loved performing. But Hailee's parents wondered if she would stick with her new **hobby**.

CALIFORNIA GIRL

Hailee Steinfeld was born on December 11, 1996, in Los Angeles, California. Her mother, Cheri, is an **interior designer**. Cheri's background is Filipino and African American. Hailee's father, Peter, is a physical trainer. Hailee is the baby of the family. Her brother Griffin is three years older than she is. Growing up, the two were very close. Griffin loved sports, especially racing cars. Hailee was always there to cheer him on.

Hailee was a cheerleader for eight years.

Hailee was born and raised in the San Fernando Valley in California.

Hailee's family always supported her as she bounced from one hobby to the next. As a child, she tried horseback riding, tennis, basketball, cheerleading, and dance. But she still wanted to do more.

A NATURAL PERFORMER

Hailee started taking acting classes at Cynthia Bain's Young Actor Studio. Her family was surprised! Hailee was a natural actress and loved her classes. She had finally found what she loved to do.

People started to notice Hailee's work. She got a few roles in television commercials. Hailee was getting used to acting in front of the camera. Her mother encouraged her to try new things.

Hailee has always been close with her parents and brother, Griffin.

Hailee Says:

"Be yourself. Believe in what you know and not what others say about you."

Hailee tried out for a role at an arts center in Thousand Oaks, California. It was a play called *The Witch Academy*. Hailee got the role of a witch named Morgana. In October 2009, Hailee performed in front of her first live audience. But her biggest performance was soon to come.

CHAPTER 2
AWARD WINNER

Ethan and Joel Coen are two major **directors** in Hollywood. In 2009, they decided they wanted to remake the western film *True Grit*. They wanted to make a movie that was true to the original novel by Charles Portis. The brothers had already **cast** Oscar winners Jeff Bridges, Matt Damon, and Josh Brolin. But they were still looking for their young star.

THE BIG BREAK

Hailee heard about the **casting call** from her cousin. She sent in an audition tape. About five weeks went by. Hailee was called in for three auditions. Finally, she learned she had landed the role of Mattie Ross. Her character wants to track down the man who shot her father.

Hailee beat out fifteen thousand girls to win the role of Mattie Ross.

Hailee with her *True Grit* costars Josh Brolin *(left)* and Jeff Bridges

PLAYING MATTIE

Hailee was willing to try anything. This helped her as an actress. To play Mattie Ross correctly, Hailee had to learn how to ride horses and shoot a gun. On her way to Texas to shoot the film, she read the book the script was based on. One of Hailee's biggest challenges was the dialect. Her character was a farm girl in the late 1800s. The directors wanted all the actors to sound like they came from the correct time and place for the story.

Hailee received the Best Young Actress honor at the Critics Choice Movie Awards in 2010.

Hailee Says:

"We will both stop at nothing to get what we want." —on her character, Mattie Ross

A STRONG START

Hailee had landed her first role in a major motion picture. She was only thirteen. Her dedication to learning her role and hard work paid off. Hailee won fourteen awards for her performance. These included the Toronto Film Critics Association Award and the Young Artist Award. She was also nominated for an Academy Award for Best Supporting Actress. Hailee was proud of her work. And she was just getting started.

CHAPTER 3
WORK AND FRIENDSHIP

Before her acting career took off, Hailee went to local elementary and middle schools. She liked school and was a good student. But Hailee was bullied in middle school. Also, her work schedule often conflicted with her school schedule. Her parents decided to homeschool her through high school.

STAYING IN TOUCH

As an actress, Hailee travels all over the world to film movies and TV shows. This means she misses out on a lot of experiences with her friends, like going to prom or graduation. Hailee doesn't have a lot of time to see her friends in person. They try to stay connected through group chats and phone calls. When she is in the same town as her friends, they like to hang out and watch movies.

Taylor Swift and Hailee worked together to create Hailee's "Bad Blood" character, The Trinity.

Hailee attends a charity event in 2010.

Hailee has some famous friends, like Taylor Swift and Selena Gomez. They are professional performers as well. They understand Hailee's dedication to her job and her busy schedule.

MUSICAL PALS

Hailee worked on Taylor Swift's music video for the song "Bad Blood." It was a fun way for the friends to combine work and play. The video is shot like a spy movie. Using special effects, Hailee played a **trio** of characters known as The Trinity. They save Taylor's character, Catastrophe, after she is hurt by a fellow spy. The Trinity nurses

Hailee Says:

"I realized in middle school that it was impossible to make everyone happy."

Hailee takes a selfie with her pal Taylor Swift.

Catastrophe back to health. Hailee had a lot of fun working with her friend. The video went on to win Best Video of the Year at the 2015 MTV Music Awards. It also won Best Music Video at the Grammys.

CHAPTER 4

PITCH PERFECT PERFORMANCE

Hailee had always loved to sing, but her acting career took up most of her time. In 2015, she was able to combine her two talents in the movie *Pitch Perfect 2*. For once, Hailee was playing a character that was similar to herself.

A NEW CHALLENGE

Hailee's character, Emily Junk, wants to prove she can sing in order to join the a cappella group the Bellas. Hailee loved the role. She saw it as a way to prove that she could do more than act. She would return to the role in the final movie in the series, *Pitch Perfect 3*.

> Hailee Says:
>
> **"As a musician, it's my story, my voice, my face."**

Hailee *(second from right)* acts in a scene with her *Pitch Perfect* costars.

After *Pitch Perfect 2* came out, Hailee released her debut single, "Love Myself." Her fans loved its upbeat message about believing in yourself. Hailee continued to work on her first full-length album. She decided to put out an EP called *Haiz*. It had four fun tracks. In 2016, she released a new version of her second single, "Rock Bottom." It was remixed by the funk rock band DNCE.

Hailee's fans call her Haiz. The nickname inspired the title of her EP.

Hailee's singing career has taken off in recent years. Here, she performs at the 2018 Grammy Awards ceremony.

ON HER WAY

In 2018, Hailee joined singer Charlie Puth on his Voicenotes tour. They began their tour in Toronto, Canada, and ended in West Palm Beach, Florida. Along the way, they played thirty-two different cities around the United States. Hailee loved listening to her fans sing her songs along with her at concerts. She knew she'd found one more calling.

TIMELINE

1996 Hailee Steinfeld is born on December 11 in Tarzana, California.

2009 Hailee is cast in the movie *True Grit*.

2010 Hailee is nominated for an Academy Award for Best Supporting Actress.

2015 She helps her friend Taylor Swift make the "Bad Blood" music video.

Reveals her singing voice in the movie *Pitch Perfect 2*.

Is signed to Republic Records.

Puts out her first single, "Love Myself."

Releases her first EP, *Haiz*.

2016 Stars in the coming-of-age film *The Edge of Seventeen*.

2017 Releases the new single "Let Me Go."

2018 Tours with Charlie Puth.

BOOKS

Kane, Bo. *Acting Scenes & Monologues for Kids!* Volume 2. Burbank, CA: Burbank, 2017.

Mattern, Joanne. *Hailee Steinfeld.* Hockessin, DE: Mitchell Lane, 2017.

VanVoorst, Jenny Fretland. *Acting.* Minneapolis, MN: Jump!, 2016.

WEBSITES

Children's Theater
childrenstheatre.org
Uses extraordinary theater experiences to inspire and educate children.

Hailee Steinfeld
haileesteinfeldofficial.com
Hailee's official website. Provides fans with the latest information on the star.

The National Theater for Children
nationaltheatre.com
This program brings live educational theater to children.

INDEX

Published in 2019 by Enslow Publishing, LLC.
101 W. 23rd Street, Suite 240, New York, NY 10011

Cataloging-in-Publication Data

Names: Santos, Rita, author.
Title: Hailee Steinfeld: actress and singer / Rita Santos.
Description: New York : Enslow Publishing, 2019. | Series: Junior biographies | Audience: Grades 3-6 | Includes bibliographic references and index.
Identifiers: ISBN 9781978503069 (pbk.) | ISBN 9781978502086 (library bound) | ISBN 9781978503076 (6pack)
Subjects: LCSH: Steinfeld, Hailee—Juvenile literature. | Actors—United States—Biography—Juvenile literature. | Singers—United States—Biography—Juvenile literature.
Classification: LCC PN2287.S6775 S26 2019 | DDC 791.4302/8092 B—dc23

Printed in the United States of America

To Our Readers: We have done our best to make sure all website addresses in this book were active and appropriate when we went to press. However, the author and the publisher have no control over and assume no liability for the material available on those websites or on any websites they may link to. Any comments or suggestions can be sent by e-mail to customerservice@enslow.com.

Photos Credits: Cover, p. 1 Jon Kopaloff/FilmMagic/Getty Images; pp. 2, 3, 22, 23, 24, back cover (curves graphic) Alena Kazlouskaya/Shutterstock.com; p. 4 Jeff Kravitz/FilmMagic/Getty Images; p. 6 Jon Bilous/Shutterstock.com; p. 7 Jason LaVeris/FilmMagic/Getty Images; p. 10 Angela Weiss/Getty Images; p. 11 Jason Merritt/Getty Images; p. 14 Chelsea Lauren/WireImage/Getty Images; p. 16 Frazer Harrison/Getty Images; p. 18 Photo 12/Alamy Stock Photo; p. 20 Brad Barket/Getty Images; interior page bottoms (theatre seats) ecco/Shutterstock.com.